Cat Food Re

Easy Recipes to Make Your Cat Happy and Healthy

Kristie Duran

Table of Contents

Chicken & Carrots Entrée 5

Moist Kitty Morsels 6

Tuna & Corn Meal Thumbprint Treats 7

Tender Broccoli & Trout Meal 8

Sardine & Turkey Meatloaf for Cats 9

Kitty Meal for Cats with Diabetic Issues 10

Eat Like a Pup Stew 11

Feline Raw Feast 12

Rice & Mackerel Dinner 13

Salmon & Broccoli Dinner 14

Carrots & Tuna Meal 15

Pumpkin Cat Treats 16

Cheese & Tuna Balls 17

Chicken, Zucchini & Squash Dinner 18

Chewy Cat Treats 19

Salmon & Egg Dinner 20

Kitty Cat Breakfast 21

Turkey & Tuna Meal 22

Kitty Trout Treats 23

Yummy Kitty Dessert 24

Soft Cheese Cat Treats 26

Catnip & Tuna Treats 27

Chicken Veggie Kitty Stew 28

Mackerel & Egg Kitty Treats 29

Sardine & Oatmeal Kitty Breakfast 30

Liver & Rice Patties 31

Chicken & Rice Meal 32

Kitty Salad 33

Pork Kitty Meal 34

Fishy Freezer Cat Treats 35

Chicken & Spinach Cat Treats 36

Beef & Alfalfa Dinner 37

Sardine & Milk Treats...38

Tuna & Milk Treats...39

Catnip & Tuna Crouton Treats...40

Broccoli & Chicken Entrée...41

Rabbit & Veggie Stew 42

Chicken & Carrots Entrée

Makes 1 Serving

Preparation time: 15 minutes + cooling time

Ingredients:

- 1 cup of chicken, cooked
- 1/3 cup of mashed carrots, steamed
- Chicken broth, low salt

Directions:

1. First, place all ingredients in food processor along with a few tbsp. chicken broth.

2. Crumble or puree ingredients till mixture looks like pate-style canned cat food. Then, add a bit more broth if you need it. Don't let the mixture get soupy, though.

3. Allow food to cool down fully and serve.

☐

Moist Kitty Morsels

Makes 24 Treats

Preparation time: 25 minutes

Ingredients:

- 1/2 lb. of turkey or beef, ground
- 1 finely grated carrot, small
- 1 tbsp. of grated cheese, mild
- 1 tsp. of brewer's yeast, gluten-free
- 1 tsp. of catnip, dried
- 1/2 cup of breadcrumbs, whole wheat
- 1 beaten egg, large
- 1 tbsp. of tomato paste, low salt

Directions:

1. Preheat the oven to 350F. Grease a baking sheet lightly.

2. In medium mixing bowl, combine meat, cheese, carrot, breadcrumbs, brewer's yeast and catnip.

3. Add tomato paste and beaten egg. Combine well. Then, use your hands to roll mixture into balls the size of walnuts or close to it. Place balls on baking sheet.

4. Bake in 350F oven for 13-15 minutes, till meatballs are firm and brown. Allow the balls to completely cool before you serve some to your cat.

5. Store in container with airtight lid in refrigerator. You can freeze these treats as well, for up to two months.

☐

Tuna & Corn Meal Thumbprint Treats

Makes Multiple Servings

Preparation time: 35 minutes + cooling time

Ingredients:

- 1 x 5-oz. can of tuna, packed in water, drained partially
- 1/2 cup of corn meal, white
- 1/2 cup of flour, all-purpose
- 1/2 cup of water, filtered

Directions:

1. Preheat the oven to 350F firstly. Then, spray your cookie sheet with non-stick cooking spray.

2. Mix the ingredients together till you have formed one ball.

3. Break tiny pieces off the ball. Roll them into little balls. Place them on the sprayed cookie sheet.

4. Flatten the balls with your fingers, just as if you were making holiday thumbprint cookies.

5. Bake in 350F oven for five to six minutes.

6. Flip the treats over. Bake for five minutes more.

7. Lastly, allow to cool fully before feeding to your cat. Store leftovers in a container with a tight-fitting lid in the refrigerator.

☐

Tender Broccoli & Trout Meal

Makes 1-2 Servings

Preparation time: 1/2 hour

Ingredients:

- 1 cup of trout, cooked fully
- 1 egg yolk, cooked
- 1 tbsp. of steamed broccoli, finely chopped
- 2 tbsp. of oil, sunflower

Directions:

1. Combine the ingredients in a food processor.

2. Puree till blended well. Serve.

3. Leftovers may be stored in fridge for two to three days.

☐

Sardine & Turkey Meatloaf for Cats

Makes 17 meals

Preparation time: 1 & 1/2 hours

Ingredients:

- 2 lbs. of ground beef, organic
- 2 lbs. of ground, boneless, skinless turkey thighs
- 2 lbs. of ground chicken organs, mixed
- 4 oz. of squash, prepped, organic
- 2 oz. of mixed berries: blackberries strawberries, blueberries, raspberries, organic
- 2 oz. of broccoli, organic
- 2 cans of packed in water sardines
- 2 oz. of kale, organic

Directions:

1. Preheat the oven to 350 degrees F.

2. Shred squash with cheese grater.

3. Puree the broccoli, squash, sardines, kale and berries.

4. Place the ground meat in large-sized bowl.

5. Add pureed fruit and vegetable mixture to meat mixture. Incorporate well.

6. Place mixture in ceramic or glass muffin or loaf pans. Bake at 350F for 1 hour. Allow to fully cool.

7. Divide baked food in 17 portions with juice included.

8. Remove a couple days' worth at once and place in refrigerator. Freeze the rest. When feeding, allow the food to warm to room temperature.

Kitty Meal for Cats with Diabetic Issues

Makes Multiple Servings

Preparation time: 35 minutes

Ingredients:

- 1 & 1/3 cups of ground turkey or chicken
- 4 cups of white rice, cooked
- 4 eggs, medium
- 2 tbsp. of oil, corn or soy
- 1/8 tsp. of salt, iodized
- Optional: 1 tsp. of parsley or a bit of grated carrot

Directions:

1. Mix all ingredients in large-sized bowl. Serve to your cat raw if she will eat it that way.

2. If not, bake the mixture at 300F for 15-20 minutes. Allow it to cool. Offer to cat again.

3. Leftovers can certainly be kept in the refrigerator for 2-3 days.

☐

Eat Like a Pup Stew

Makes Multiple Servings

Preparation time: 1 hour & 15 minutes

Ingredients:

- 1 chicken, whole
- 2 cups of rice, brown
- 6 celery stalks
- 8 scrubbed, unpeeled carrots, medium
- 1 crown of broccoli, small
- 1 handful of green beans

Directions:

1. Wash the chicken. Place in large pot, then cover with filtered water.

2. Slice the veggies in small pieces. Add to the pot. Add the rice, too.

3. Cook till chicken is nearly falling off bones, and veggies have become tender.

4. Carefully debone chicken completely. Chicken bones splinter when eaten and can cause damage to your cat's intestines, if ingested.

5. Pour stew in food processor. Chop or blend till mixture is coarse and roughly bite-sized for your cat. Cool and serve. Freeze extra in individual-meal-sized zipper top bags.

□

Feline Raw Feast

Makes Multiple Meals

Preparation time: 15 minutes + cooling time

Ingredients:

- 2 cups of rolled oats, cooked
- 2 eggs, medium
- 4 cups of chicken or turkey, ground
- 2 tbsp. of oil, flax seed or olive
- 1 tsp. of vegetable, fresh, like peas, squash, zucchini or carrots

Directions:

1. Stir the egg into cooked oats. Allow to cool a bit if oats are still hot.

2. Mix in the rest of the ingredients. Separate what your cat will eat within a few days and then freeze the rest promptly. Putting the mixture in meal-size zipper top bags will make in easier when it comes to thawing and serving.

☐

Rice & Mackerel Dinner

Makes 1-2 Servings

Preparation time: 20 minutes

Ingredients:

- 1 cup of mackerel, canned
- 1 tbsp. of oil, sunflower seed
- 1 tbsp. of brown rice, cooked
- 1 to 2 tbsp. of beef or chicken broth or filtered water

Directions:

1. Combine the ingredients in a food processor.

2. Puree till blended well. Serve promptly.

3. You can place leftovers in refrigerator for up to 3 days.

☐

Salmon & Broccoli Dinner

Makes 1-2 Servings

Preparation time: 15 minutes

Ingredients:

- 1 can of salmon, de-boned
- 1 tbsp. of mashed broccoli, cooked
- 1/4 cup of breadcrumbs, whole wheat
- 1 tsp. of brewer's yeast

Directions:

1. Combine all your ingredients in medium bowl.

2. Stir together well, then serve.

3. Refrigerate leftovers for two to three days.

☐

Carrots & Tuna Meal

Makes 1-2 Servings

Preparation time: 20 minutes

Ingredients:

- 1/2 cup of chicken, cooked
- 1 can of tuna, packed in oil
- 1 tbsp. of mashed carrot, cooked

Directions:

1. Combine all the ingredients in food processor.

2. Puree till blended well. Serve.

3. Refrigerate leftovers up to three days.

☐

Pumpkin Cat Treats

Makes 20+ Servings

Preparation time: 40 minutes + cooling time

Ingredients:

- 1 x 4-oz. can of salmon, without added oil or salt
- 1/2 cup of oats, old-fashioned
- 1/3 cup of pureed pumpkin
- 1 egg, medium
- 2 tbsp. of oil, avocado

Directions:

1. Preheat oven to 325F.

2. Add oats to food processor. Blend into fine-textured flour.

3. Open salmon can. Drain off excess fluid.

4. Combine oat flour from step 2 with avocado oil, egg, pumpkin and salmon. Combine well.

5. Form into little cookies. Place on cookie sheet. Bake in 325F oven for 25 to 30 minutes, till firm.

6. Allow treats to cool fully before you serve treats to your kitty. Break them in smaller sized pieces if you need to. Leftovers can be stored in refrigerator in airtight container for three to four days.

Cheese & Tuna Balls

Makes 1-2 Servings of Treats

Preparation time: 40 minutes + cooling time

Ingredients:

- 1 small can of tuna packed in oil
- 2 tbsp. of breadcrumbs, unseasoned
- 1 well-beaten egg, large
- 3 tbsp. of cheese, grated

Directions:

1. Preheat the oven to 350F.

2. Mash ingredients together well till they form a mixture with a texture like paste.

3. Shape the mixture in balls. Place on a greased cookie sheet.

4. Bake at 350F for 20-22 minutes, checking frequently to see if they are finished cooking. When treats are firm and golden-brown in color, they are done.

5. Allow to cool before you serve to your cat.

☐

Chicken, Zucchini & Squash Dinner

Makes Multiple Servings

Preparation time: 1 & 1/4 hours

Ingredients:

- 1 lb. of chicken
- 2 zucchini, medium
- 2 squash, yellow
- 2 cups of rice, brown

Directions:

1. Wash the chicken. Place in large pot, then cover with filtered water.

2. Slice the veggies in small pieces. Add to the pot. Add the rice, too.

3. Cook till chicken is nearly falling off bones, and veggies have become tender.

4. Carefully debone chicken completely. Chicken bones splinter when eaten and can cause damage to your cat's intestines, if ingested.

5. Pour stew in food processor. Chop or blend till mixture is coarse and roughly bite-sized for your cat. Cool and serve. Freeze extra in individual-meal-sized zipper top bags.

☐

Chewy Cat Treats

Makes about 50 treats

Preparation time: 1 & 1/4 hours + cooling time

Ingredients:

- 1 egg, large
- 1 x 4-oz. jar of brown rice and chicken baby food or canned cat food
- 1/4 cup of parsley, chopped coarsely
- 2 tsp. of oil, olive
- 2 tbsp. of water, filtered
- 1 cup of flour, brown rice
- 1/2 cup of well-cooked white or brown rice
- Optional: 1 tbsp. of additional wet canned food, 1 tbsp. catnip

Directions:

1. Place oven rack in center slots of oven. Preheat to 325F. Line cookie sheet with baking paper. Set it aside.

2. In medium mixing bowl, whisk the egg, wet food or baby food, water, oil and parsley together.

3. Add cooked rice and flour. Stir and incorporate well. Mixture should be thick but still spreadable.

4. Spread the mixture on cookie sheet, making a large rectangle about 1/3" in thickness.

5. Bake in 325F oven for 12-15 minutes.

6. Remove cookie sheet from oven. Allow to rest till you can handle it safely. Slice the soft dough in small bite-size pieces. Return to oven and bake for eight more minutes. Remove from oven.

7. Allow treats to completely cool. Serve. Certainly, store in container with tight-fitting lid in refrigerator.

Salmon & Egg Dinner

Makes 1 Serving

Preparation time: 45 minutes

Ingredients:

- 1 hard-boiled, chopped egg, large
- 1 cup of canned salmon

Directions:

1. Take a large-sized bowl. Add the egg.

2. Boil fish for 10-20 minutes, till flesh is soft. Remove all bones.

3. Add fish meat to large bowl. Mix all ingredients well.

4. Heat in microwave oven. Serve lukewarm.

☐

Kitty Cat Breakfast

Makes 1 Serving

Preparation time: 25 minutes + cooling time

Ingredients:

- 1 tbsp. of milk, nonfat dry
- 3 eggs, medium
- 3 tbsp. of cottage cheese, small curd
- 2 tbsp. of grated vegetables, like squash, carrots, broccoli, etc.

Directions:

1. Mix the dried milk with a bit of water.

2. Add eggs. Beat together thoroughly.

3. Pour mixture into non-stick fry pan. Cook over med-low till done.

4. Flip like you would a pancake. Spread veggies and cottage cheese over one half of cooked surface. Then fold up as you might an omelet. Allow the meal to cool, then cut into bite size pieces and serve.

☐

Turkey & Tuna Meal

Makes 28 meals

Preparation time: 1/2 hour

Ingredients:

- 4 x 6-oz. cans of tuna, packed in water
- 2 cups of rice, cooked
- 1 pound of turkey livers
- 12 chopped parsley sprigs with removed stems

Directions:

1. Chop parsley finely. Transfer to large bowl.

2. Bring large-sized pot of filtered water to boil. Drain chicken livers in sieve over sink. Rinse them well and drop them into the boiling water.

3. Allow the water to return barely to boil. Remove pan from heat. Cover it. Allow the turkey livers to poach for four to five minutes. Drain them well. Rinse in cold, filtered water. Chop in a food processor. Add to bowl with the parsley.

4. Drain the tuna, then add to the mixture, with the rice.

5. Mix, then mash mixture fully till combined well. Fill storage bags or plastic, lidded containers. Actually, refrigerate for up to seven days or freeze in meal-size portions for as long as three months.

Kitty Trout Treats

Makes 125 treats

Preparation time: 45 minutes

Ingredients:

- 1 x 10-oz. can of undrained trout
- 1 beaten egg, large
- 2 cups of flour, whole wheat
- Cookie cutter, small

Directions:

1. Heat the oven to 350F. Line a cookie sheet with baking paper.

2. Pulse the undrained trout in food processor. Do chop it as finely as you possibly can.

3. In bowl of stand mixer, combine the chopped trout, beaten egg and flour, till the dough has formed. If dough seems to be dry, add water as needed. If the dough does feel too wet or sticky, add a little more whole wheat flour. The dough, when ready, should not be sticky, but it should be tacky.

4. Next, roll out the dough on floured work surface till it has a thickness of about one-quarter inch.

5. Use a 3/4" cookie cutter with a fun shape, if you have one, to make the treats.

6. Place the raw treats on baking paper-lined cookie sheet. Then, bake in 350F oven for 18-20 minutes or so. When they are crunchy and a bit browned, they are done.

7. Allow the treats to cool fully before you serve them to your cat.

8. Leftovers can be stored in a container with a lid for up to two weeks.

Yummy Kitty Dessert

Makes 1-2 Servings

Preparation time: 40 minutes

Ingredients:

- 1 large-sized can of milk, evaporated (do not use Milnot®)
- 2 tbsp. of plain yogurt, full-fat
- 2 tbsp. of real mayonnaise
- 1 tbsp. of Karo® syrup, light
- 1 pkg. of gelatin
- 1 beaten yolk from large egg
- 1 cup of water, filtered

Directions:

1. Mix the milk, mayo, syrup and yogurt together fully.

2. Next, bring a cup of filtered water to a boil. Mix in the gelatin. Set it aside.

3. Then, mix the egg yolk with a bit of milk mixture. Beat thoroughly.

4. Add water and gelatin to the milk mixture. Beat thoroughly.

5. Add in the egg yolk mixture. Beat together well.

6. Pour into plastic bowl with lid. Place in the refrigerator.

7. Serve when desired. Pudding will last for 12-14 days when covered and left in fridge.

☐

Surprise your feline with delicious cat treats!

You can actually get a dog to do almost anything if you offer him a treat. But cats are more different than dogs, in many ways. Still, most cats will enjoy treats if you test different flavors and find their favorites.

These recipes for homemade cat treats are easy to make, and you'll enjoy rewarding your cat anytime. From tuna to sardines, you can serve these tasty treats as you desire.

Every cat has her own food preferences, and unless your cat is new to your home, you probably know some of her favorites. Be sure your treats contain a good deal of moisture, too, since cereal and grain-based treats aren't as healthy for cats. Always supervise your kitty when she is enjoying treats.

☐

Soft Cheese Cat Treats

Makes 24 Treats

Preparation time: 1 hour + cooling time

Ingredients:

- 3/4 cup of flour, white
- 3/4 cup of cheddar cheese shreds
- 5 tbsp. of Parmesan cheese, grated
- 1/4 cup of yogurt, plain
- 1/4 cup of corn meal

Directions:

1. Preheat oven to 325F.

2. Combine yogurt with the parmesan and cheddar cheeses in medium bowl.

3. Add corn meal and flour together to yogurt and cheeses. Mix thoroughly till it forms a dough.

4. Knead dough into ball. Then, use rolling pin to roll out to 1/4" thickness.

5. Cut dough in 1" pieces Place on lightly-greased cookie sheet.

6. Bake for 20-22 minutes in 325F oven till treats have JUST firmed up. Allow to cool on cookie sheet for several minutes. Remove treats to wire rack and allow them to completely cool before you feed them to your cat.

Catnip & Tuna Treats

Makes Multiple Treats

Preparation time: 1 hour + cooling time

Ingredients:

- 5 oz. of drained tuna, packed in water
- 1 egg, large
- 1/2 cup of flour, all-purpose
- 1/2 cup of corn meal
- 1/4 cup of flour, wheat
- 1/4 cup of water, filtered
- 1/2 tsp. of catnip, chopped small if not already
- 1/4 cup of wheat germ

Directions:

1. Preheat the oven to 350F.

2. Line baking sheet using foil.

3. Mix ingredients in large-sized bowl till combined well.

4. Form mixture into a dough. It will have a sticky consistency, and that's okay.

5. Place the dough on floured work surface.

6. Pull off little pieces of the dough. Roll them in small-sized balls.

7. Press dough balls till they are about the size of nickels. Place on foiled baking sheet.

8. Bake for 20-22 minutes in 350F oven.

9. Allow to completely cool before serving.

10. Indeed, if you have leftovers, you can store in the refrigerator for a few days.

Chicken Veggie Kitty Stew

Makes Numerous Servings

Preparation time: 55 minutes

Ingredients:

- 2 cups of rice, brown
- 8 scrubbed, un-peeled carrots, medium
- Chicken, boneless
- 1/4 cup of green peas
- 1 handful of green beans

Directions:

1. Wash chicken inside and out. Place in large pot. Cover with water.

2. Cut vegetables in small-sized pieces. Add to pot.

3. Add rice to pot.

4. Cook mixture till chicken has become soft and vegetables become soft enough for your cat to eat.

5. Pour all stew in large sized food processor and blend well.

6. Allow mixture to cool. Serve in your cat's bowl.

□

Mackerel & Egg Kitty Treats

Makes 18 Treats

Preparation time: 25 minutes

Ingredients:

- 1/2 cup of drained and crumbled mackerel, canned
- 1 cup of breadcrumbs, whole-grain
- 1 tbsp. of bacon grease or vegetable oil
- 1 beaten egg, large
- 1/2 tsp. of brewer's yeast, gluten-free

Directions:

1. Preheat the oven to 350F. Then, grease a baking sheet with butter or spray.

2. Combine the ingredients and mix them thoroughly. Drop the dough in 1/4-tsp's on baking sheet with an inch between them.

3. Bake in 350F oven for 8-9 minutes. Cool the biscuits before serving.

4. Cover leftovers and store in refrigerator.

Sardine & Oatmeal Kitty Breakfast

Makes 1-2 Servings

Preparation time: 10 minutes

Ingredients:

- 1 can of oil-packed sardines
- 2 tbsp. of mashed carrot, cooked
- 1/3 cup of oatmeal, cooked

Directions:

1. Combine all the ingredients in medium bowl.

2. Mash the ingredients together well. Serve.

3. Leftovers can certainly be stored in your refrigerator for up to three days.

☐

Liver & Rice Patties

Makes 1 Serving

Preparation time: 20 minutes

Ingredients:

- 1/2 cup of rice, cooked
- 1/4 cup of pureed liver
- 2 or 3 chopped parsley sprigs

Directions:

1. Mix all the other ingredients with the drained tuna.

2. Roll three or four balls in your hands. Form them into patties. Serve.

3. Leftovers can certainly be stored in the fridge for two to three days.

☐

Chicken & Rice Meal

Makes 1-2 Servings

Preparation time: 10 minutes

Ingredients:

- 1/2 cup of chicken, cooked
- 1 can of tuna, packed in oil
- 2 tbsp. of rice, brown
- 1 tbsp. of mashed carrot, cooked

Directions:

1. Combine ingredients in food processor.

2. Pulse till blended well. Cool and serve.

3. Leftovers can certainly be refrigerated for up to three days.

☐

Kitty Salad

Makes 2-3 Servings

Preparation time: 10 minutes

Ingredients:

- 1/4 cup of zucchini, grated
- 1/2 cup of alfalfa sprouts, chopped
- 1/8 cup of stock, fish or chicken
- For garnishing: 1/8 tsp. of catnip, minced

Directions:

1. Combine ingredients in medium bowl. Toss well.

2. Sprinkle catnip over the top and serve.

3. You can store leftovers in container in refrigerator for two to three days.

☐

Pork Kitty Meal

Makes 1-2 Servings

Preparation time: 5-10 minutes

Ingredients:

- 1/4 tsp. of oil, salmon or olive
- 1 oz. of cooked potato, peeled
- 1 tsp. of pasta, cooked
- 3 oz. of pork, whole meat

Directions:

1. First, mix all ingredients together in food processor and serve as desired.

2. You may store leftovers in refrigerator for a couple days.

☐

Fishy Freezer Cat Treats

Makes 12-16 Servings, depending on ice cube tray used

Preparation time: 20 minutes + freezing time

Ingredients:

- 1 can of salmon or tuna, water-packed
- 1/2 cup of water, filtered
- 1 ice cube tray, plastic

Directions:

1. Tip undrained canned fish in food processor. Add water. Blend together well.

2. Fill a zipper top plastic bag with fish mixture. Cut small-sized hole in one corner. Fill ice cube tray with mixture.

3. Freeze till cubes are solid. Remove them from tray. Certainly, store in airtight container in freezer for up to six months. Thaw to serve.

Chicken & Spinach Cat Treats

Makes Multiple Servings

Preparation time: 1 & 1/4 hours + cooling time

Ingredients:

- 1/2 lb. of chicken thighs, skinless, boneless, steamed
- 1 cup of spinach leaves, fresh
- 1 cup of oats, quick-cooking
- 1 egg, brown
- 1 tbsp. of catnip, organic
- 1/4 cup of flour, all-purpose

Directions:

1. Preheat oven to 350F. Line a cookie sheet with baking paper.

2. Steam chicken till it has cooked fully through. If you prefer, you can use tuna or salmon. Allow the chicken to cool for 15-20 minutes before proceeding to step 3.

3. Place chicken, spinach, oats, egg & catnip in food processor. Pulse on a low setting till mixture has blended together well. It should be somewhat chunky but mostly smooth. The texture should be like wet sand.

4. Pour mixture in medium or large bowl. Add flour. If you actually like, you may add a dash of sugar or salt to tweak the flavor.

5. Knead dough by hand till it isn't sticky anymore. Place on floured work surface.

6. Using your rolling pin, create rectangle from dough that is about 1/2" in thickness. Use a small-sized cookie cutter or pizza cutter to create shapes from the dough.

7. Place treats on cookie sheet. Bake in 350F oven for 18-20 minutes, then remove sheet pan from oven. Allow the treats to cool fully and then give them to your feline pal.

Beef & Alfalfa Dinner

Makes 2-3 Servings

Preparation time: 15 minutes + cooling time

Ingredients:

- 1 cup of beef, ground
- 1/2 cup of steamed rice, brown
- 6 tbsp. of alfalfa sprouts, minced
- 3/4 cup of cottage cheese, small curd

Directions:

1. Brown ground beef in non-stick fry pan. Drain well. Allow to fully cool.

2. Mix ingredients in medium bowl. Serve.

3. Leftovers can certainly be refrigerated for two to three days.

☐

Sardine & Milk Treats

Makes 24 Treats

Preparation time: 25 minutes + cooling time

Ingredients:

- 7 oz. of sardines, mashed
- 1/2 cup of wheat germ
- 1/4 cup of milk, non-fat, dry
- **Directions:**

1. Mix the ingredients well. Roll mixture in 24 small-sized balls.

2. Place balls on a greased baking pan and flatten them using a fork.

3. Bake in 350F oven till they turn brown. Don't let them burn.

4. Lastly, remove treats from oven and allow to cool before serving.

☐

Tuna & Milk Treats

Makes Multiple Servings

Preparation time: 45 minutes + cooling time

Ingredients:

- 1/4 cup of milk, skim
- 1/2 cup of flour, whole-wheat
- 1/2 x 6-oz. can of oil-packed tuna
- 1 tbsp. of oil, vegetable
- 1 egg, large

Directions:

1. Preheat the oven to 350F. Spray baking sheet using non-stick spray.

2. Place tuna in medium bowl. Flake apart the chunks, then use a fork to mash them well.

3. Add flour to tuna. Continue mashing and mixing.

4. Pour milk into tuna and flour mixture. Add egg and oil. Stir together well, till ingredients have mixed together thoroughly.

5. Use a teaspoon to scoop out one portion of the dough. Divide portion in two and roll them into balls. Repeat with the remainder of dough.

6. Place the dough balls on prepared baking sheet.

7. Place baking sheet in 350F oven for 10 minutes. Remove treats from the oven, then allow them to cool completely before serving to your cat.

8. The remainder of treats can be stored in resealable container or bag in refrigerator or freezer.

Catnip & Tuna Crouton Treats

Makes Multiple Servings

Preparation time: 30 minutes + cooling time

Ingredients:

- 1 x 5-oz. can of tuna, water-packed, drained
- 1 tbsp. of flour, coconut
- 2 tbsp. of oil, olive
- 1 egg, large
- Catnip, dried, as much as you desire
- Water, filtered – use only as needed if dough is dry

Directions:

1. Preheat oven to 325F. Line a cookie sheet with baking paper.

2. Combine ingredients in food processor till smooth. Pinch dough pieces into the shapes of croutons.

3. Bake in 325F oven for 10-15 minutes. Check them so they don't overcook or burn.

4. Remove from oven. Allow the treats to cool before serving to your feline pal.

5. Leftovers can be stored in containers with lids in the refrigerator.

Broccoli & Chicken Entrée

Makes 1-2 Servings

Preparation time: 20 minutes

Ingredients:

- Chicken broth, low salt
- 1 cup of chicken, baked or broiled
- 1/4 cup of steamed & mashed broccoli
- 1/4 cup of steamed & mashed carrots

Directions:

1. Place a few tbsp. of broth in food processor along with other ingredients.

2. Crumble or puree ingredients till it looks like pate-style cat food. Then add broth gradually till you have a smooth mixture. Don't let it become runny.

3. Serve after food has cooled fully.

4. Leftovers can certainly be stored in the refrigerator for a couple days.

☐

Rabbit & Veggie Stew

Makes 4-5 Servings

Preparation time: 1 hour & 5 minutes

Ingredients:

- 1/2 pound of rabbit meat, de-boned
- 1 tsp. of oil, olive
- 1 dash each of rosemary, thyme and parsley
- Vegetable stock, unsalted
- 3/4 oz. of peas, celery, carrots and sweet potatoes, chopped

Directions:

1. Sauté the rabbit meat in oil in pot on medium heat.

2. Sprinkle rabbit with the herbs. Add the vegetable stock. Then, bring to boil.

3. Reduce the heat to med-low. Allow meat to cook fully through.

4. Add the chopped vegetables. Simmer for 45 minutes or so.

5. Next, allow to cool down to room temperature before serving.

6. Optional: you can run the mixture through a food processor to make it easier for your cat to eat. This will also help her to eat the vegetables.

7. Leftovers can be stored in refrigerator for two to three days, or frozen.

Made in United States
Troutdale, OR
08/06/2023

11854376R00024